TAROT FOR BEGINNER WITCHES

Learn How To Read Tarot Cards For Divination and Spellcasting

JULIE WILDER

Contents

Also by Julie Wilder — v

Don't Forget Your Free Book! — 1

PART I
A PRACTICAL INTRODUCTION TO TAROT

1. My Magical Philosophy — 5
2. Tarot Myths — 17
3. Tarot History — 27
4. How to Acquire Your Tarot Deck — 31
5. Storing and Charging Your Tarot Deck — 37

PART II
HOW TO START READING TAROT CARDS

6. Tarot Basics — 47
7. How to Shuffle, Draw and Interpret Your Tarot Cards — 51
8. How To Talk To Your Intuition With Tarot Cards — 61
9. Secret Questions Tarot Ritual — 65
10. Small (Yet Mighty) Tarot Spreads — 67

PART III
HOW TO CAST SPELLS WITH TAROT CARDS

11. How To Cast Spells with Tarot Cards — 73
12. A Sentimental Tarot Love Spell — 85
13. A Powerful Tarot Money Spell — 91

Also by Julie Wilder — 99

Also by Julie Wilder

What Type of Witch Are You?
How to Become A Witch
Why Didn't My Spell Work?
Beginner Witch's Guide to Grimoires
Tarot for Beginner Witches
Simple Moon Magic
White Witch Academy Books 1-3 Boxed Set

Don't Forget Your Free Book!

If you want to learn more ways to practice simple, secular witchcraft, be sure to pick up a **copy of this free book of spells**, and my **free Beginner Witch Starter kit** with printables, correspondences, meditations, and magical journaling prompts. Use the link below to get both of those!

https://whitewitchacademy.com/freebies

And if you're into oracle cards, check out my updated deck, **the How To Become A Witch oracle deck**—perfect for spell casting and divination. No other magical tools necessary! **It's everything you need to start casting powerful spells TODAY!**

https://whitewitchacademy.com/modern-goddess-oracle-card-deck

PART I
A PRACTICAL INTRODUCTION TO TAROT

My Magical Philosophy

My Magical Philosophy

Hi! I'm Julie Wilder, writer, tarot reader, entrepreneur, oracle deck creator, and personal development junkie, and a practicing secular witch. I've read tarot cards professionally in the past, but now I mostly read for myself. I've written four other books about witchcraft, and I have more coming. I've included a list of the other books in this series at the end of this book. You can also find links to those books on my website at www.whitewitchacademy.com/books.

My goal in everything I write is to empower others to connect with their power and magic—and yes, I believe every single one of us is inherently powerful. We are all energetic beings, which means we can all tap into the energy in and around us to cast spells and perform divination with tarot cards.

Tarot is my absolute favorite magical tool, and that makes this book extra-special to me. This little guide is perfect for someone who is interested in learning practical ways to harness the power of tarot cards in their witchcraft practice!

The Way I Teach Witchcraft and Tarot

I'm not going to tell you how to practice your witchcraft—in this book, or any of the books I write—because I believe magic is highly personal. There is no "right" or "wrong" way to be a witch. Us, witches, have to decide what exactly we want out of our witchcraft—and tarot—practice.

For me, I get really excited when I see my tarot spells manifesting. I also love the feeling of reading my tarot cards and sensing the truth of the card's message. That's why I use tarot in my magic.

Maybe you are drawn to tarot for other reasons. It doesn't matter to me why you're here—I'm just glad you are! Tarot has gone mainstream in recent years, and I'm thrilled to see lots of people interested in learning about this beautiful magical tool! When it comes to the tarot and witchcraft community, the more the merrier!

You might not agree with everything in this book, and that's totally fine. I believe it's important to really chew on things before you accept them. Blazing your own trail is what witchcraft is all about.

People often ask me how I got into witchcraft. The answer is pretty simple. I owe it all to tarot cards. My friend had a deck of tarot cards and she did a three-card reading for me. It was super basic—past, present, future—that kind of thing.

Neither of us knew much about tarot cards, so we had to pause the reading to do an internet search for the meaning of each card. We had a lot of fun, and I was shocked by how much that super-basic tarot reading rang true to me.

After that, I was hooked.

Totally hooked.

I bought myself a tarot deck and started experimenting with single card draws and the spreads suggested in the guidebook that came with the deck. Next, I started adding my own interpretations to my tarot readings. Soon, I moved on to creating my own tarot spreads and doing more free-form rituals, like using the tarot cards to talk to my intuition.

From there, I added bits of magic to my tarot practice. I would cleanse my cards with selenite, Himalayan pink sea salt, or with the light of the new moon. I also explored using a variety of magical techniques to charge my cards. I used rose quartz to prepare my cards for love-themed tarot readings or

I'd lay a few coins on top of my deck before drawing cards for a reading about my finances.

After getting pretty familiar with the different cards in my tarot deck, I started selecting certain cards to represent my desire during spells and on my altar—the Emperor to help me be more organized in my entrepreneurial endeavors, the Magician to help me manifest big goals, and the Nine of Pentacles for confidence and financial abundance.

These tarot spells proved to be incredibly powerful, and I almost always include a tarot card or two in my spell casting. I'll tell you about the different ways you can draw on the magic of tarot to super-charge your spells in this book.

So what about you?

What drew you to tarot cards? What are you most curious about learning with your cards? Keep that in mind as you read over what is and isn't covered in this book. I want to make sure this book is right for you. It's written for anyone who is interested in learning the basics of tarot and how to use a deck of tarot cards for divination and magic.

Here's What I'll Cover In This Book:

- Overview of the Major Arcana, the Minor Arcana, and the suits.
- Why you don't have to follow traditional tarot rules, myth busting, and a

discussion on gatekeeping in witchcraft. (No, you definitely don't need to be gifted your first tarot deck!)
- Answers to common tarot questions like "What do 'jumping' cards mean," "How do I cleanse my tarot deck," and "What if the tarot deck gives me bad news?"
- Tips for performing insightful tarot readings
- How to prepare your space, your cards, and yourself for performing a tarot card reading intuitively
- The process of choosing and arranging tarot cards for powerful spellcasting including money and love spells
- Fun, unconventional tarot spreads to try
- How to use tarot to connect to your inner wisdom and manifest your deepest desires
- Suggestions for witchcraft altar setups using tarot cards

I'm a practical person and this book is going to be short, concise, and full of actionable practices so you can start drawing cards today.

What I Don't Cover:

I want to be super clear about this up-front

before diving further into this book. I'm not going to talk about the meanings of each of the seventy-eight tarot cards, and I have a couple of reasons for not doing this.

First, these definitions are SUPER easy to look up online. All you have to do is type the name of the card into your internet search engine to find a variety of thoughtful and insightful card meanings. Most of the tarot decks you can buy also include a guidebook. You can use that to look up the meanings as you go, and this is a perfectly valid way of performing tarot readings.

The second reason is that I don't want you to feel limited by my interpretations of the cards. My approach to witchcraft is highly intuitive, and I believe everyone has a deep well of power, strength, and ancient wisdom inside of them. This book will teach you to access that inner power. For me, tarot isn't about straight-up memorizing definitions that may or may nor resonate with you. It's about blazing your own path and using your unique view of the world to cast some serious spells.

Secular Witchcraft

I write about and practice secular magic. It's the kind of witchcraft that can be paired with any religion or belief system. It doesn't matter if you're an atheist, a Buddhist, a Christian, a Muslim, or any other religion.

For a long time, I thought you had to be a Wiccan to be a witch. Not true! Wicca is a religion with its own set of rules, gods and goddesses, and traditions. Wiccans often consider themselves witches, but not all witches identify as Wiccans.

You might hear the term "Pagan" thrown around when you're talking to other magic-minded people. Paganism is an umbrella term used for many nature-based religions. Note the word religion. Paganism is a religion, just like Wicca, or Christianity, Hinduism, Islamism—you get the idea. Some Pagans also consider themselves witches, but not all witches identify as Pagans.

Make sense?

Secular witchcraft is magic that isn't based in any religion. Secular witches work with energy and the spiritual realm to create change in the physical world. Their practice is not guided by a set of rules, books, or specific gods or goddesses.

Maybe you've heard the Wiccan Rede which states that any magic you do to others will come back on you "threefold."

In secular witchcraft, you create your own system of ethics and moral guidelines. I choose not to curse people because I've found it to be a waste of my valuable energy. It doesn't make me feel better when someone suffers—even someone I don't like.

You might disagree, and there is room for that in secular witchcraft! I won't tell you what to do. You make the rules, and you take responsibility for your actions.

So let go of any preconceived beliefs you have about witchcraft and tarot! Open your mind to the possibilities and let your intuition guide you. You can tap into the ancient, powerful magic of the universe your way.

How to Trust Your Intuition

My witchcraft is led by my intuition. Likewise, my tarot practice is also completely intuition-based.

I recently learned that not everyone has a deep connection to their intuition.

If this is you, and you find your eyes glazing over every time people say things like, "Let your intuition guide you" and "Trust your intuition," don't sweat it! Let me explain what I mean when I talk about intuition.

For me, "intuition" refers to that wise, comforting, sometimes tough-love voice you hear whenever you face a new issue, conflict, thought, or belief. Some people refer to their intuition as an "instinct" or a "hunch." Sometimes your intuition will warn you when you're in danger. Other times, your intuition will push you to take a risk.

Have you ever walked into a room and thought something like, "This place feels homey" or "This cafe feels sad and depressing?" That's probably your intuition talking.

When you're introducing a new magical tool into your witchcraft practice—such as a new tarot deck—you'll need to make many intuitive choices. You'll have to decide what kind of deck to buy, how to "break it in," and how to use it.

To do this, you can ask other witches for advice. You can read books about tarot cards like this one. You can research the topic on the internet. But in the end, all that matters are the choices *you* make regarding your tarot and your witchcraft.

I encourage people to always trust their intuition above the opinions and recommendations of others. No one knows you like you!

The tricky thing about intuition is that it isn't the only voice echoing around the labyrinth of your mind. You might also hear the voices of fear, past trauma, or social conditioning.

Note: most witches won't actually hear a voice. I'm referring to the thoughts, feelings, and images that zip through your mind.

For example, let's say you go on a date with a kind, interesting, attractive person. You have a lot of fun laughing and sharing stories with each other.

You feel a real connection to this person. Then you leave your date knowing that you want to see this person again. That "knowing" could be your intuition nudging you toward your desires—a healthy, joyful relationship.

Then you get home and you second guess yourself. You have thoughts like, "This person is too good to be true," "I should end this thing before I get hurt," or "I don't have time for a relationship right now." Personally, I would classify these thoughts as fear-based, and I don't think they are likely coming from your intuition.

Here's The Major Difference:

Your intuition will always be the voice that feels bold, expansive, and full of possibility.

Your fear-based voice is the opposite. It will urge you toward choices that seem safe, small, familiar, and contracting.

What if you still aren't sure?

Sometimes I feel like I'm being pulled in two different directions, and both directions feel equally wonderful. When this happens, it's hard to understand what your intuition is telling you.

In my experience, the solution is to just pick one. Make a choice and don't overthink it. Then take notice of your thoughts and feelings following your decision. Do you feel excited, hopeful, and buoyant? Do you regret your choice immediately after you make it? If so, why? Are you scared of the growth that might come from your new path, or are you sad because you realized you only picked this course of action based on other people's perception of you?

Pay attention to everything you think and feel as you lean further into your choice. If you do this often enough, you'll notice patterns. You'll learn to recognize what it feels like when you're being guided by your intuition.

That's how I define intuition in a nutshell. It's not as mystical or woo-woo as some people make it out to be. It's just about listening to yourself!

Whatever you do, don't beat yourself up for ignoring your intuition. Even the most magical, enlightened witch will not maintain "perfect alignment" to themselves and the universe at all times. Noticing those intuitive nudges takes practice and lots of trial and error. Be gentle and loving to yourself.

I believe I have a decent connection to my intuition, but I know that sometimes I still make choices out of fear. So what? Making mistakes is what being human is all about. Embrace it. Each decision (right or wrong) reveals a lesson that will deepen your magical practice.

Yes, you are magical.

Yes, you are powerful.

Yes, you have everything you need inside of you RIGHT NOW to use your tarot cards to perform insightful tarot readings and bad-ass witchcraft spells.

Seriously.

So if that all sounds good to you, read on! Let's make some tarot magic!

Tarot Myths

When I first started learning about tarot, I discovered there were a lot of "rules" involved. The more I worked with my tarot cards, the more I realized that a lot of these rules weren't necessary. Some of them felt more like beliefs to keep witches out of the tarot practice than actual guiding principles. This is called "gatekeeping," and it sucks. I've seen this happening in other witchy disciplines, and I do my best to dispel these myths whenever I can. Don't let other witches discourage you from exploring your natural abilities.

Note: There are some branches of witchcraft that you must be born into or require a formal initiation. I'm not talking about that stuff when I talk about gatekeeping in the magical community. I'm talking about practicing tarot as a secular witch.

Along those same lines, there are also culture-specific or religious-based practices that have made their way into witchcraft. For example, "smudging" is a Native American practice, while "smoke cleansing" is a witchcraft practice. For that reason, I am careful of this distinction and I don't use those terms interchangeably. That's where you get into culture appropriation, and as secular witches, I believe it's important for us to keep the conversation going and be as respectful to other cultures as we can.

If you want to know more about culture appropriation and the differences between a Wiccan, a pagan, and a secular witch, you can check out "What Type of Witch Are You?" You can find the link to that at www.whitewitchacademy.com/books.

In terms of tarot, I believe reading tarot cards is highly personal, and I don't think it's cool to tell people it has to be done a certain way or that you have to be a certain kind of person to be able to do it.

In this chapter, I've gathered up all the myths I've heard thrown around over the years, and I'll give you my two cents on why they aren't true!

You have to be psychic to read tarot cards

False! You do not have to be psychic to read tarot cards, nor do you have to be psychic to be a witch. All you need to do is look at the imagery of each card, familiarize yourself with the card meanings, and then decide how they relate to your specific circumstance. Anyone can do this. Literally, anyone.

Also, can we all take a second to ruminate on the word "psychic"? What even *is* "psychic"? For me, it sounds like a label. People love labels—and that's fine—but I think this label can actually be applied to everyone. I don't think it's reserved for a select few.

I believe we are all at least a little "psychic." I associate being "psychic" with being "intuitive" and that we're all born with this "sixth sense." Being psychic is when you think about your friend, and then they choose that moment to call you. It's when you "feel" someone's eyes on you when your back is turned. It's when you can tell if someone is lying to you.

This inner knowing is where a lot of your power comes from as a witch, and you deepen your connection with that part of yourself every time you sit down to practice your witchcraft. Activities like journaling, meditating, scrying, tarot reading, candle gazing, moon baths, and being in nature all strengthen your natural intuitive abilities.

If you don't include divination in your magical practice, you're not a real witch

Nope, not true either. Tarot cards are a form of divination, and divination is just one small part of witchcraft. Some witches choose not to practice divination altogether for a variety of reasons. Maybe they don't want to know the future because it spoils the fun. Maybe it gives them anxiety if the cards say something bad.

Whatever the reason, it's totally fine to not use tarot cards or any other form of divination in your witchcraft practice. You're still a witch, and a darn powerful one.

Tarot is fortune telling

Mmmm... kind of? Sure, you can use tarot cards to predict the future and tell your fortune, but the tarot can do so much more. I've used tarot cards to talk to my spirit guides, connect with my intuition, understand my feelings, detect the energies in my relationships, identify self-sabotaging issues within myself, receive guidance on decision-making, and, of course, spellcasting! Fortune telling is just the beginning. In this book, we'll explore some of my favorite unconventional ways to use your tarot cards.

Tarot cards are magical

Yes, and no. Some witches disagree with me, but

I don't think tarot cards are inherently magical. It's ink that was printed onto little rectangles of paper by a printing company.

I do, however, believe that tarot cards can hold power to be used in spells and divination spreads. That power doesn't come from the ink on the paper. I believe it comes from the way YOU interact with the cards. When you look at, hold, or shuffle tarot cards, your energy will respond to the colors, texture, symbolism, numbers, and words on each card. The meaning you place on the cards and the way a card makes you feel sends energy into the card. That charges the cards with power.

For example: if you draw the Empress card and you think about the traditional meaning of the card —abundance, sensuality, and wild feminine energy. That thought will sink into that card, charging it with the particular energy. Then let's say you notice some feelings coming up within you as you gaze at the imagery. Maybe you feel excited, blissful, or courageous. Those feelings will also settle into that card, giving it more power.

You might also notice some memories floating up from your subconscious when you look at the card. In the Rider-Waite deck, the Empress card depicts a woman with long, wavy blonde hair. Maybe that reminds you of the time you and your best friend bleached your hair in high school, which makes you laugh. That playfulness—though not typically associated with the card—will settle into the card.

I believe that the mixture of energy of your personal associations adds magic and power to the cards. It's not about the actual artwork, it's about *your personal connection* to the artwork.

Your tarot readings need to be 100% accurate all the time

I don't believe tarot readings are accurate all the time for two main reasons.

First, tarot is a snapshot of your current situation and guidance on the future IF you stay on your current path. If you make a different decision, you'll get a different outcome. Nothing is set in stone.

Second, your tarot readings won't be 100% accurate all the time because you're human, which means you're not perfect. You'll get things wrong, and that's OK. Sometimes I've thought my tarot cards were predicting a romantic weekend with someone special, only to find myself binge-watching Netflix in my yoga pants. Did that mean I read the cards wrong? Personally, I've stopped judging myself on the accuracy of my tarot readings. I choose to believe that any message I receive is for a purpose. For example, maybe I received that particular message about a romantic weekend for a reason. Maybe that reason was to bring to my attention my deep desire to connect with someone so I can honor that need within myself and start dating in earnest.

The other thing I do when I get a tarot reading "wrong" is to look back and see if the cards make more sense in hindsight. Once, I kept getting the Three of Swords (heartbreak, sadness, despair), the Ten of Pentacles (family, leaving behind a legacy, creating something that lasts), and the Tower (a powerful shakeup). I believed they were telling me I'd have a conflict with one of my family members or close friends. The Tower card made me think it would be something sudden and unexpected. I wondered if this conflict would be linked to a health issue or accident.

This didn't happen.

Instead, my landlady texted me out of the blue and told me I had forty-five days to find a new place to live because she was selling the building. Looking back at the tarot readings I performed around that time, it makes perfect sense. I was sad to leave my month-to-month rental and had to find a more permanent place to live. It was sudden and required me to step up and have a personal breakthrough. In hindsight, those cards explained the situation perfectly.

That being said, sometimes you look back and you still can't make sense of it. Do yourself a favor and let it go, my witchy friend. Let it go.

There are good cards and bad cards

No tarot card is all bad. Even the more traditionally "negative-focused" cards carry a hopeful message of guidance to help you out of a sticky situation. The Tower is all about tearing down old structures so you can build it back even stranger. The Death card is about the end of a cycle and the beginning of something new and exciting.

Also, what's so bad about those "icky" feelings and awkward life moments? Sure, they can be uncomfortable, but they are also often cathartic. We watch movies with sad endings because we want to experience the highs, lows, and lessons of a story. We read horror books in the dark under the blankets because, on some level, we enjoy being scared. As long as you are experiencing these emotions safely, you are probably strengthening your emotional toughness.

Tarot can do the same thing. The traditionally negative cards can allow a witch to connect with their shadow self and have a good old-fashioned wallow. Who wants to watch rom-coms all day every day? A variety allows us to feel the complex beauty of the human experience.

There is a right way and wrong way to read tarot

When I first started learning tarot, I looked all over the internet for the "correct way" to shuffle and draw tarot cards, and guess what? I couldn't find a standardized technique. I found videos of tarot readers working with decks of tarot cards, got some tips from a few tarot-loving friends, and read lots of blog articles that seemed to describe everything about tarot EXCEPT how to shuffle and draw cards.

Over time, I developed my own methods of pulling cards. I'll share that with you in this book so you can have a starting place. After you get more comfortable with the cards, I'd encourage you to try new ways of shuffling—perhaps you cut the deck four times. Maybe you flip one card over at a time as you do a reading. You might totally hate that "tingling hand" method I use.

What one tarot reader does may not work for another, and one method is no more accurate or "legit" than another. Don't fall into the trap of thinking you have to follow the rules to get this tarot thing right. In some cases, conforming to the mainstream methods of divination and spellcasting makes you feel stifled and separated from who you are.

Each card only means one thing

Um, no. This isn't math, people, it's art! It's

magical storytelling! Two different tarot readers might draw the exact same cards in the exact same spread and interpret them in completely different ways.

I think that's one of the coolest things about tarot. It's not about memorizing card meanings and regurgitating the info. As a tarot reader, you get to look from card to card and see how they all come together in one story. It's highly subjective.

Think of it as if you're looking at a painting created by a skilled artist. How would you describe that painting? What details would catch your eye? What would it make you feel? It's unlikely two people are going to interpret a painting in exactly the same way. We experience the world differently based on who we are, what we've gone through, and what our goals are. All of that is going to affect the way you interpret your cards.

Tarot History

I'm going to keep this short because this book is mostly about actionable ways to get you started using your tarot cards for divination and spell casting. However, if YOU love learning about the origin and evolution of the tarot, check out the books "The Essence of Tarot" and "Tarot for Beginners." You can find links to those here: www.whitewitchacademy.com/resources.

Ready for a super-brief history lesson? Here it goes:

No one is 100% sure where tarot came from. Some historians believe it can be traced back to ancient Egypt. The characters and ideas in the Major Arcana have shown up in hieroglyphics on the walls of ancient Egyptian religious structures representing a human's path to enlightenment or possibly a way to communicate with the gods.

Later on, a form of tarot appeared in Italy as a card game played at parties—purely for entertainment, with no occult overtones. Around the same time in Spain, a love-based divination card game gained popularity. From there, the tarot developed into a fortune telling tool that was practiced by nobles throughout Europe. At some point, the occultist community started using tarot in their magical practices, and that brings us to the version of modern-day tarot we are familiar with!

These days, a tarot deck is typically a seventy-eight card system for divination, decision-making, goal-setting, manifesting, magical spells, personal development, and fun.

The most popular tarot deck is the Rider-Waite deck, sometimes called the Rider-Waite-Smith deck (to give recognition to the talented artist). In 1909, an artist named Pamela Smith was commissioned to illustrate this seventy-eight card deck by a man named Arthur Edward Waite.

This deck is rich with imagery. It's a great beginner deck because most of the pictures clearly convey the message of each card without the tarot reader having to memorize the meanings.

The Rider-Waite deck has inspired many deck creators with its imagery, and hundreds of modern tarot decks have been made based on artists' reimaginings. You'll see this if you check out the decks at your local bookstore. I bet there will be at least a couple that are variations of the Pamela Smith and Arthur Edward Waite's original tarot deck.

Kim Krans' The Wild Unknown Tarot deck is one of the beautiful modern decks that helped tarot breakaway from the Rider-Waite system and go mainstream. This deck takes a fresh approach to the seventy-eight cards by using plants, animals, and nature scenes to convey the meaning of each card. Rather than using the relatively darker imagery of the Rider-Waite deck (like the Devil card with a horned creature holding two people in chains and the Tower card with people jumping out of a flaming building), Krans' deck uses lighter, less-religious illustrations. This deck resonated with lots of people who were curious about tarot and witchcraft. The Wild Unknown Tarot deck appeared all over social media and since then, other artists have stepped up to create some truly magical decks. I'll share some of my favorites later in this book.

How to Acquire Your Tarot Deck

There are hundreds of different tarot decks you can choose from, a notion that is both exciting and slightly overwhelming. No tarot deck is better than another.

The benefit of using the Rider-Waite deck or a "Rider-Waite"-based deck is that many books and websites will refer to the specific imagery of this deck. This is helpful when you're learning and familiarizing yourself with card meanings.

If you don't like the illustrations of the traditional Rider-Waite deck, Biddy Tarot makes a beautiful deck that uses similar imagery but still maintains its own aesthetic style. It uses the colors purple, white, black, and yellow with a design that relies on clean, crisp shapes to depict the cards rather than the intricate drawings of the Rider-Waite deck. For example, the seven of pentacles in the Rider Waite and Biddy tarot decks both show a person staring down at their growing crops.

All traditional tarot decks have the same seventy-eight cards. Most decks are split into two main groups: the **Major Arcana and the Minor Arcana**. Within the Minor Arcana, there are four suits: **pentacles, wands, cups, and sword**s. No matter what version of tarot cards you use, you'll be able to read the cards by the name of the card. Each deck works the same way, and each card means the same thing.

For example, the Fool in the Lumina deck is depicted as a woman dancing joyfully with a deer standing beside her. The Fool in the Rider-Waite deck is a jester-type man with a dog, walking dangerously close to a cliff.

Both cards embody innocence, youth, and potential recklessness, even though they are illustrated in dramatically different ways.

Where to Get A Tarot Deck:

If you're looking to acquire a tarot deck, you can get one from several places. Some people will tell you that your first tarot deck should be given to you by someone else.

That's all well and good if you have a friend or family member who practices tarot. In that case, you can ask if they have a spare deck they'd like to pass on to you.

The problem is you might not know anyone who practices tarot. You might not even feel comfortable telling anyone about your newfound interest in tarot because you're worried about being judged or ridiculed.

I don't subscribe to this belief, and it bums me out to think of all the would-be witches who gave up learning about tarot and magic because they didn't know anyone with a spare tarot deck!

You don't have to be or do anything to be "worthy" of a tarot deck.

You don't have to take a course or prove your abilities before you can call yourself a tarot reader.

If you want a tarot deck, don't wait for someone to give you a deck. Go out and buy one!

Choosing A Tarot Deck:

Because there are so many options for tarot decks, I recommend you do a little research before you go out and buy one. Pinterest, Instagram, and other social media platforms have lots of gorgeous decks made by indie creators. Sites like Kickstarter and Indiegogo are also great places to find unique tarot decks by artists. If you search YouTube, you'll find entire channels devoted to rating and reviewing new tarot decks. Amazon and Etsy have a lot of great deck options—particularly for traditionally published tarot decks.

I like buying decks from metaphysical stores because I love supporting small businesses, and the shop owners can offer recommendations on the different decks.

Here are some things to look for when buying a new tarot deck:

-Imagery that you resonate with.

Some decks are very detailed and full of symbolism—such as the Rider-Waite deck, the Biddy Tarot deck, and the Lumina deck. This is great for beginners because the pictures can help you better understand and connect with the meaning of each tarot card. Other decks take a "less is more approach" like the Simple Tarot. The cards in that deck include straightforward designs and keywords so you can use them like tarot flashcards!

-Thickness of cardstock

If you're mostly going to be using your tarot cards on your altar or for spells, you might want to get a deck with super-thick card stock. If you're planning on performing tarot readings, go with a deck that has thinner, more flexible cardstock so you can easily shuffle.

-Price

Tarot decks sell at all different price points, so

don't let the cost stop you! Mass produced decks are usually cheaper ($20-$40) while indie decks tend to be more "high end" ($40-$120). You might be able to find some used decks on eBay or at thrift stores.

What if you don't want to invest in a deck yet?

Maybe you're brand new to tarot and you're not ready to spend money on your own deck yet. That's totally fine! I recommend getting seventy-eight notecards (or pieces of paper) and making your own set of tarot cards. Label each card with a card name and use them as you would a regular tarot deck. Another option is to look up card designs on the internet, print out the images, and glue them to your notecards. This is usually OK even with copyrighted images as long as it's for your personal use only.

My Favorite Decks

The Rider-Waite deck—the most popular with the most widely recognizable imagery.

The Simple Tarot by Angie Green—a color-coded learner deck with outlined designs and keywords. The starter kit includes a guidebook, stickers, cheat sheets and more!

The Wild Unknown Tarot by Kim Kranz—an inexpensive deck with hand-drawn artwork. It has a sort of messy, hipster vibe that I love. If you're into yoga, you'll enjoy the references to yogic breathing techniques and terms like "dharma" sprinkled throughout the guidebook. This deck will be a little different than other tarot decks because it refers to the four knights as "sons" and the pages as "daughters."

The Lumina Deck by Inner Hue—a deck with vibrant watercolor designs of people and animals. This one is pricier, but the cardstock is thick and sturdy and the artwork is jaw-dropping. I love using these cards on my altar.

Biddy Tarot—an inexpensive "pocket-sized" deck with clean Rider-Waite-inspired designs.

The Crystal Unicorn Tarot—another Rider-Waite-inspired deck with bright colors and unicorns! It reminds me of Lisa Frank designs in the best way possible.

Tarot in Translation—a beautiful deck that includes keywords, poetic phrases and symbolism.

For links to these decks, check out my website at www.whitewitchacademy.com/resources.

Storing and Charging Your Tarot Deck

Make Friends With Your New Tarot Deck

When you first open your card deck, I believe it's a similar energy to meeting a new friend! I like to make a little ritual out of it, and I invite you to try it out the next time you get a new tarot deck (or any magical tool).

Create a peaceful, magical atmosphere in your space such as playing your favorite music playlist, diffusing lavender essential oil, or finding a spot near a flowing river—wherever you'd like to have a joyful meeting with a new friend.

Once you're settled in, open up your tarot deck and go through the cards one at a time. Hold each one and examine the imagery.

You might want to have a journal or grimoire

nearby so you can jot down your initial thoughts and feelings as you're getting acquainted with your deck.

If you feel called, go ahead and talk to each card if you want! Ask what it has to teach you, and notice the thoughts and feelings that come up within you immediately after. Often, that's how your intuition will speak to you.

Yes, I know talking to your tarot cards is kind of weird, but wherever. No one's judging you!

There are two main reasons I like to "break in" my new tarot decks in this way. The first reason is that I believe the more bonded you feel to your tarot cards, the more powerful your readings will be. The second reason is that while you're doing this ritual, you may be able to sense the energy of the deck.

Sensing A Tarot Deck's Current Energy

As you get more familiar with your tarot deck, you might start to detect its shifts in energy. Sometimes a deck's energy will change if someone else shuffles the cards. Sometimes its energy will change if it's been knocking around at the bottom of your backpack for a few days.

Even a brand new tarot deck will come to you holding a variety of different energies. Think about all the people and places the deck has come into contact with on its way you—shop employees, post office personnel, wooden crates, shipping trucks, etc.

That's a lot of energy! Sometimes, you might like that hodgepodge of energy and you want to preserve it as long as you can in your cards. Other times, you'll decide to clear out the old, lingering energy and start with a blank slate.

The best way I know how to sense a deck's residual energy is to notice what happens in your head and your heart while you're interacting with the deck. You might look over the cards of your new deck and find yourself thinking unwanted thoughts, such as stewing about an old fight with your best friend, or replaying the moment you found a parking ticket on your windshield. If this happens, I recommend doing some energy work on the deck before doing a reading.

Changing Your Tarot Deck's Energy

Energy changes all the time, so if you suspect your deck needs to be cleansed of any unwanted energies, you can modify that energy by cleansing it, charging it, or doing both!

How to Cleanse Your Tarot Cards

White Light Meditation

There are a lot of different ways you can do this, but the simplest method is a traditional "White Light Meditation."

Close your eyes and listen to your breath. Notice your inhales and exhales, notice the stability of the earth underneath you as you hold your tarot deck in your hands.

When you feel grounded, visualize a white light moving down from the sky. This is the cleansing white light of the universe. Allow it to wash over you and your cards and feel it float into the surrounding space. As it fills the area, it will gently guide the unwanted energy away from you and your tarot deck.

I recommend doing this meditation for about five to ten minutes, but feel free to go longer or shorter as you feel guided. When you feel like you've done the job, open your eyes.

Crystal Cleansing

Set crystals on your stack of cards to cleanse them and leave them there for at least ten minutes. If I'm not using my cards, I'll leave a crystal on them overnight. Selenite, amethyst, and smoky quartz work well for this. I use this method when I'm tired, crabby, or I don't want to use my own energy for whatever reason. All the energy for this cleansing method comes right from the crystal!

Incense Cleansing

If you have any incense or herb bundles, light

them up and allow each card to pass through the smoke to cleanse it. I also like to do this when I'm "making friends" with my deck. Make sure you practice proper fire safety when you light incense, and remember to ventilate the room you're burning incense in. Don't burn incense around children, pets, or anyone around you with small lungs.

Sea Salt Cleansing

Another simple way to cleanse energy is to sprinkle a handful of sea salt onto your cards. I did this between tarot readings when I was performing tarot at a party. When so many energies are interacting with your deck, sea salt is a quick, reliable way to wipe away any lingering energy of the previous client.

How to Charge Your Tarot Cards

Once you have cleansed your tarot deck and you're starting from a place of neutral energy, you may want to take it a step further and charge the cards with energy to match the intention of your spell or reading.

Charging a space is a simple concept, and I'm sure you've done it many times throughout your life without even knowing. Have you ever hosted a birthday party? What did you do? Turn on some fun, high-energy music. You might have put up streamers, balloons, or some kind of eye-catching decorations to give the room a celebratory feeling. You make sure all the food and drinks match the joyful, vibrant mood of the party—maybe you use colorful plates or add fun garnishes to the drinks.

All of those things are examples of how we intuitively "charge" a space to make it feel fun and celebratory in honor of someone's birthday.

Think about that when you want to charge your own space. Identify what kind of energy your spell or tarot spread needs. For example, you'll want to make the energy of your deck feel warm, cozy, and romantic for a love reading. Put on some love songs, dim the lights, and spray your favorite perfume in the room.

If you're performing a tarot reading or spell to increase your psychic abilities, you'll want to cultivate the energy of quiet, peaceful meditation. Diffuse your favorite essential oil into the air (or use one that is associated with psychic awareness like jasmine or rose oil). Put on some soothing instrumental music. Drink a cup of tea and breath in the steam. Lavender, dandelion, or chamomile are great for this intention.

The alternative to cleansing and charging your space is to find a space that already holds the energy you desire for your spellwork. To do this, simply make a list of all the places that come to mind when you think of your intention.

For a money spell, you might want to place your cards in a place that feels abundant, such as a lush forest. Other places that could be ideal for this might be: in a beautiful hotel room, on the kitchen table as you munch on a delicious cheese plate, or in front of a gorgeous fountain.

Storing Your Tarot Cards

When my tarot cards aren't in use, I like to wrap them up in an altar cloth to keep them safe and organized. I intentionally chose an altar cloth over a box because boxes don't travel well. With a square shaped cloth, I can wrap them up and throw them in my tote bag on my way out the door. Then I'll pull them out when I need some midday guidance or I'll place a card on my desk to set my intention for the day. Whenever I need to create a magical mini altar in the middle of my busy day, I just lay out my cloth and quiet my mind as I connect to the energies of the cards. My deck of tarot cards and my altar cloth—which is usually a pretty patterned "fat quarter square" from the fabric store—can become my portable personal spiritual oasis.

I also love using an altar cloth to wrap my cards because I'll often toss in a few crystals, a sprig of rosemary or lavender, or a handful of sea salt in the cloth. That way, your tarot cards will always be ready for use the next time you unfold your cloth.

What if you get a deck and don't feel a connection to it?

This has totally happened to me. I'll get super

excited about a tarot deck I see on social media. Then I'll order it and stalk my tracking information until it arrives in my hands. The problem happens when I open the deck up, shuffle it, and begin my "bonding" ritual. I won't feel as enthusiastic about the deck anymore. I don't know exactly why this happens. It could be an energetic mismatch or buyer's remorse. Whatever the reason, I'll find myself reaching for my other go-to decks rather than my sparkly new deck! When this happens, I usually find someone to pass the deck onto—a friend, family member, or co-worker. One time I gave one of my decks to my car mechanic's wife because she had a budding interest in tarot and it just felt right. Giving something away feels so good. It keeps your energy flowing and makes someone else smile!

PART II
HOW TO START READING TAROT CARDS

Tarot Basics

The Major Arcana

There are twenty-two cards in the Major Arcana. These cards are considered the "trump" cards in the deck. Whenever these cards show up in a tarot card spread, pay special attention.

These Major Arcana cards are usually numbered from zero, the Fool tarot card, to twenty-one, the World tarot card. The Major Arcana cards take you on a journey, similar to Joseph Campbell's "Hero's Journey," going through all the different phases of life, different obstacles, and different opportunities for growth. The Fool card is a card of new beginnings and the World card represents completion and celebration.

If you're dealing with a difficult life situation, you might want to try this simple ritual.

Separate the twenty-two Major Arcana cards out from your tarot deck and ask, "What energy do I need to successfully navigate this tricky situation?" Your cards will give you the answer through the loving, powerful characters of the Major Arcana.

The Four Minor Arcana Suits

Pentacles

The pentacles suit represents the earth element. The tarot cards in this suit all deal with the physical world and material things—finances, wealth, your belongings, your home, and sometimes your career or family. Seeing a pentacle card show up in a tarot reading could be a sign that you're starting to turn your hopes and dreams into reality!

Wands

The wands suit represents the element of fire. This wild and wonderful suit is all about inspiration, creativity, passion, and movement! The wands tarot cards usually point to your deepest ambitions, goals, desires, and passions. Wands cards might ask, "What is your purpose?" or "What are you living for?" No matter what the answer is, a wand tarot card showing up in a tarot spread is almost always a sign to go for it! Don't stop now. Your burning ideas are waiting to become realized! You've got this. All you have to do is believe in yourself.

Cups

The cups suit represents the element of water. When you pull a cups tarot card, you know you're dealing with matters of the heart. More specifically, cups usually refer to issues around your emotions, feelings, and intuition. This suit can shed some light on your relationships, such as your relationships with your family, friends, lover, your higher power, or even your relationship with yourself! Many times, cups tarot cards speak directly to questions about love and romance.

Swords

The swords suit represents the air element. The tarot cards in this suit deal with thoughts and ideas. Themes of mental clarity, logic, new ideas, intellect, action, and change are addressed within the swords suit. Though there is often conflict associated with a swords tarot card, like a double-edged sword, each tarot card in this suit comes with its own solution. When you draw a sword tarot card, think fast! You likely already know the answer.

How to Shuffle, Draw and Interpret Your Tarot Cards

A lot of tarot readers use an overhand shuffle. Some use a riffle shuffle. I use a mixture of both.

An **overhand shuffle** is when you hold the deck from the bottom with one hand and then you loosely pull out a few cards from the middle of the deck with your top hand, sliding them back into the front of the deck.

A **riffle shuffle** is when you cut the deck into two piles. Then you grip both piles of the deck with your thumbs on the facing edges of the cards. Release the cards by loosening your thumbs so the cards feather down and the two piles are mixed together.

If you type "overhand shuffle" and "riffle shuffle" into YouTube, you'll get plenty of videos showing you exactly how to do those shuffling methods.

How Long Should You Shuffle Your Cards?

When you're shuffling tarot cards, it's different from when you're shuffling playing cards for a game of Go Fish. You have to "feel" when it's time to start and stop shuffling. There's no "right" amount of time to shuffle.

You shuffle until you feel called to stop. It could take one shuffle or ten. Your intuition will tell you when it's time. If you don't feel a connection to your intuition at the moment, don't sweat it. No need to overthink it. In fact, I've found my intuition is sharpest when I just follow the first thought (or hunch or instinct) that flits through my mind.

If you start thinking thoughts like "Should I stop? Did I shuffle too long? How do I know if I'm doing this right?" then take that moment to pause, breathe, and know that you are doing it exactly right. That's my philosophy, anyway. My magic gets all wonky the instant I start second-guessing and beating myself up. If you're prone to that kind of unhelpful self-talk, use the act of shuffling your tarot cards to "turn off" those thoughts. You're doing it right, OK? Trust me. You are.

My other trick for keeping my mind focused while shuffling is to repeat my question or the topic of my spread over and over in my head like a mantra. For example, if I'm doing a tarot spread on my career, I'll repeat the phrase, "I'm asking for guidance on my career, I'm asking for guidance on my career, I'm asking for guidance on my career..." If my mind still wanders (because I'm a normal human being), I'll whisper or speak my intention aloud.

The reason it's important to keep your mind on the question or topic of your tarot spread is because your mind is what will guide your hands as you flip over cards. If you are doing a career spread but you start thinking about your ex-lover as you shuffle the cards, you might end up looking at cards that explain your current love situation rather than your job prospects.

Whenever I draw cards that I can't make sense of, it's usually because my mind wandered to some unrelated topic as I was shuffling. When that happens, I bring my mind back to my original question, reshuffle the cards, and start again.

How To Draw Your Tarot Cards

I use two different methods and I make my choice based on the number of cards I plan on pulling in a spread and what my intuition is telling me to do. You might find you prefer one method over the other, or you might discover an entirely different method for drawing cards. I've learned these two methods from other witches I respect.

I've added my personal touches to each one, and I invite you to do the same.

Method A:

Cut the deck as many times as you want and lay the stacks of cards side-by-side. Turn your left hand up towards the sky and absorb the energy from the universe, your spirit guides, or your higher power. When I do this, I close my eyes and mouth something like, "Spirit guides, please guide my hand as I choose cards" or "Intuition, send your wisdom to me." I always use my left hand for this part because in magical theory, the left side of your body naturally receives energy and the right side of your body naturally projects energy.

As you hold your palm and set your intention to receive energy, pay close attention to all the sensations that follow. When I receive energy, I often feel a light pressure, a temperature change, tingling, or just a certain "knowing" that I've received energy. If you don't feel anything, that's OK. Sometimes, I don't feel any physical sensation. In that case, I'll simply decide I'm ready to draw cards. You don't need to be holding your hand up for twenty minutes!

Next, you can flip your hand over and hold it above your stacks of cards. Let your hand hover, palm down, over each card stack—one at a time. Again, notice what sensations you feel in your hand and body as you do this. Select the pile with the strongest sensation. If you don't feel anything at first, keep moving your hands over the stacks until something inside of you nudges you to pick one.

Once I pick a pile, I put it on top and slide the other stacks underneath it in whatever order I want. Now your cards are in one pile.

The last step is to draw your cards off the top of your stack and place them in the suggested tarot spread positions. This card drawing method is great if you have six or more cards to draw in a spread.

Method B:

Spread the cards out in front of you on a flat surface in a big arc. Adjust the cards so each card is visible, even if it's just a tiny sliver.

Next, hold your left hand up and wait until you feel like you've received energy into the hand (just like in method A). When you're ready, bring that hand down over your "arc" of cards and let it hover —palm down—an inch or two above the cards. Move your hand back and forth over the entire stretch of cards until you feel a sensation in your hand or a nudge to draw a card.

Do this for each card until you've drawn all your cards for your spread. This method takes a bit more time, so it's ideal if you're doing a spread with only one to three cards.

. . .

Those are the two most common methods I've come across, but use whatever method you want. There are certainly other ways to draw cards. Sometimes, I'll drop all my cards in a big messy pile and pick from there. You don't have to get all precious about this process if you don't want to. If you're new to tarot, you'll eventually discover a style that works best for you! Experiment with both methods or make up your own. There's really no wrong way to draw cards.

Jumping Cards

You might be shuffling and a card will fall or "jump" out of the deck. Congratulations, witch! You've just come across a "jumping card." Many readers believe those cards contain special messages and can add depth or context to your reading. Yes, I know, maybe the card fell out because you're clumsy or your hand slipped or whatever.

But maybe it's something more than that.

Stay open to the joyful surprise of a jumping card and feel free to use that card somewhere in the spread. If you don't have a specific spot of the card, consider using it as an "overall mood" of the spread. If you're confused about the card, make a note of it in your grimoire or journal and refer back to your spread later on. Perhaps it makes sense in hindsight.

Remember, you are totally allowed to put the card back and continue shuffling if you don't feel like that card was meant for you. Sometimes cards fall out. We live in a physical world. If it was a message, your intuition or guides will get through to you another way.

Your intuition or your magical instincts will be your most valuable asset when reading tarot cards—or doing any kind of divination. Tarot cards are literally just ink on paper. You add the magic. The messages and stories you discover through these cards are all formed from your perception of the card meanings, the energy around you, and your inner wisdom.

Reverse Cards

If you draw a card and it appears upside-down to you, you've drawn a reverse card. The reverse meaning of a card varies. Sometimes it means the opposite of the card's traditional meaning. Other times, it has the same meaning as the card right-side-up, but in a stronger, more intense way. If you get the Nine of Swords, a card of worry and anxiety, the reverse meaning is a crap ton of worry and anxiety.

If you want to know the reverse meanings of

each card, the booklet that came with your cards might have some info on that. If not, you'll be able to find the meaning online if you type in the card name and the word "reversed" into your search engine bar.

Not all tarot readers read reversed cards. I rarely do because I feel like the traditional seventy-eight card meanings provide a rich story on their own. Because of that, I make sure to shuffle so all my cards appear upright. Some tarot readers believe that reverse cards add more nuanced messages to a reading. I recommend you try out both ways and see what you like!

Positioning Your Tarot Cards

After you draw your cards, place each card in the position according to the spread you're using. Classic tarot spreads like the Celtic Cross Spread have a specific way of laying out cards. Other, more informal spreads might not offer any instructions for card placement. If you are making up your own spread or there isn't a set layout, you can position your cards in whatever way makes sense to you. Make sure you remember what question or intention you selected for each card.

When To Flip Over Your Cards

When you are flipping over your cards, you have a few choices. You can either flip them over as you draw them, or you can place them in your spread face down and flip them over one at a time as you read through your speed. When I'm reading for myself, I prefer the latter method because I like to be surprised as the story unfolds. When I'm reading for someone else, I almost always flip the cards over immediately before starting the reading so I can get an overall sense of the cards and my interpretation before I begin talking.

Interpreting The Cards

Once you've flipped over your cards, sit back and look them over. Take your time and don't immediately go for your guidebook. Sometimes the most insightful messages come to you organically. Examine the colors, settings, and characters of each card. Take in all the details and try to spot something you've never noticed before.

As you gaze over the whole spread, see if any patterns or stories rise to the surface. If there are a lot of pentacles in the reading, maybe you have material and financial matters on your mind. If you see most of the cards are in the cups suit, maybe the reading is about the relationships in your life or your feelings.

It can be helpful to keep a journal nearby to jot

down different thoughts that flicker through your mind as you start interpreting your cards. Many times, those initial thoughts, feelings, and images are how your intuition will talk to you. Once you spend a minute or two looking over the cards, go ahead and look up the card meanings in your guidebook or online! There's no shame in looking up card meanings. I still do it and I've been reading cards for years. Sometimes, I get a burst of insight from reading over someone else's interpretation of a card on a blog or book.

How To Talk To Your Intuition With Tarot Cards

You don't always have to do a formal tarot spread when you draw tarot cards. You can ask questions on the fly and pull a card or two for each answer. One of my favorite things to do with my tarot cards is to use them to talk to my intuition. I believe you can use a tarot deck to speak to any spiritual power—your intuition, your higher power, your deities, your spirit guides, or the universe.

Directions:

To begin, sit in a comfortable position and hold your tarot deck between your palms. Close your eyes. Bring your awareness to your breath. You don't have to change in any way—just notice it. Once you feel relaxed and connected to your body and breath, speak aloud (or think) your intention. For this magical ritual, your intention should include who or what power you want to communicate with and what exactly you want from the conversation. It can be something like, "Intuition, I call on you for guidance." Wait for a moment until you feel like your intention was received. Then shuffle your cards as you normally would.

Create A Space For Magic

In a perfect world, you'll want to do this ritual in a room or space where you won't be disturbed for at least fifteen minutes. I know this might be hard for some of you with roommates and families, so do the best you can. In a pinch, I've even done this ritual in an airport terminal.

Consider setting the mood with soothing music, candles, and incense. Jasmine incense is my go-to when I'm connecting with my intuition or higher power. Feel free to have a comforting drink to sip on throughout this ritual. I like to drink coffee because it makes this feel like a fun coffee date with a good friend.

Begin The Conversation

This can be as formal or as casual as you'd like. I

keep it casual—like I'm having a chat with my friend over coffee.

1. Spread your tarot cards out in front of you, face-down, in a big arc. Hold your left hand over your cards, hovering an inch or two above them.

2. Ask a question. You can ask anything you want—whatever's on your mind. I like to start with something like: "Intuition, what is the energy of the day?" or "Moon, what message do you have for me today?"

3. Move your hand back and forth over the entire arc of cards and draw a card. That's the answer to your question.

What If Your Card Answer Doesn't Make Sense?

If you look at your tarot card and have no idea what it means, sit with the card a little longer. Examine the colors of the image. Also, pay attention to any thoughts or feelings that float through your mind as you look at the card. If nothing comes to mind, look up the meaning in this guidebook or check out some tarot websites to get new insights on the card's meaning. I have a few sites I love, but when I'm really stumped on an answer, I search for websites I've never visited before.

Don't forget, you're always welcome to ask for clarification from your tarot deck—just like you would if your friend said something you didn't quite understand. You can ask something like, "What do you mean by that?" before drawing another card or two.

Continue The Conversation

Once you feel like you have your answer, go ahead and ask another question to continue the conversation. Then repeat the process of selecting a card for your answer. If you don't have any further questions, you might want to share a comment or insight with your tarot deck, intuition, or higher power. Act just as you would when having a conversation with a friend. Don't overthink your words, just speak, draw cards, and enjoy your time with your tarot deck!

Continue this conversation until you feel complete. To end this ritual, gather up your tarot cards and hold them between your palms. Thank your tarot deck, your intuition, or your higher power for talking to you.

And you're done! You can do this ritual whenever you feel like you need some guidance or company.

Secret Questions Tarot Ritual

If you're looking for a new way to experience tarot, you can try this fun variation for a daily tarot ritual.

Write down questions on strips of paper and place them in a jar. To add a witchy element to this ritual, place the jar outside in the moonlight overnight. (You can also try placing it near a window if you're not able to put it outside due to weather or if you live in an apartment, etc.)

Then sit down with your jar of questions and your tarot deck. Speak your intention aloud or in your head. Something like, "Please send me guidance on the question I draw through the cards." Then draw a question and a card at the same time. That card is the answer to your question. If it's unclear, draw a second card for clarification. You can do this with one question or continue pulling cards until you get to the end of the questions in the jar.

I love doing this tarot ritual in the morning after meditation or before I go to bed in the evening. It's a quick and simple way to add magic to my daily life.

Small (Yet Mighty) Tarot Spreads

Here are some simple tarot card spreads that can be used with your witchcraft practice!

Morning Energy Spread

This spread is a great one to create a daily ritual around. Do this spread every morning or evening to get a sense of the energy in the air and the energy you're holding that day.

Card One: Today's Energy
Card Two: My Energy

If you draw a card that freaks you out a little, take a deep breath and smile. It's all good. Just pull another card as you ask the question, "What can I do to shift this energy?" Journal about your thoughts.

Magical Dualities Spreads

Life is all about dualities, isn't it?
Summer and winter
Day and night
Joy and despair
Life and death

These next three spreads all explore the energy of duality and how it shows up in our lives. Witches know that duality is not only natural, it's beautiful. When we acknowledge and celebrate the light and dark sides of life (and ourselves), we can dance between worlds with grace and ease.

Witch's Flow of Energy Spread

This simple spread can help you claim your power through self-discovery. Allow the cards to provide you with guidance regarding what kind of energy you need to call into your life and what kind of energy you need to release. Staying in a specific energy for too long stifles growth—even if it's a positive energy. Change is necessary to rise to your best self every single day.

Card One: Attract
Card Two: Release

Intuitive Coffee Chat Spread

The name of this spread was inspired by one of my favorite activities—getting coffee and chatting with my friends! That's right, my tarot cards are totally my friends.

The thing about good friends is they always tell you the truth—even if you don't want to hear it. They usually have a good sense of what's true because they know you and they can see your blind spots. This tarot spread explores the energies you are sending out, both consciously and subconsciously. Your cards will tell it like it is. Once you know what energy you're sending out, you can choose to change it or to feed that energy. This small tarot spread may have a big impact on your manifesting magic.

Card One: What energy am I consciously sending out?

Card Two: What energy is floating around in my subconscious?

Simple Moon Energy Spread

Use this tarot card spread at the beginning of each lunar cycle to discover what energies the new moon and the full moon hold. This can help you plan your activities, rituals, and spells so you stay aligned to the moon all month long.

Card One: New Moon Energy
Card Two: Full Moon Energy

PART III
HOW TO CAST SPELLS WITH TAROT CARDS

How To Cast Spells with Tarot Cards

This idea of using cards for magic appealed to me because, for a while, I lived out of a suitcase. Let me just say it was really bothersome to have to lug all my crystals, candles, and wands through airport security.

> TSA: **Ma'am, do you have rocks in your purse?**
>
> Me: **No. (Pause) Oh, you mean my crystals? Then yes. There are indeed rocks in my purse.**

I thought, how awesome would it be to be able to perform any kind of spell with one single magical tool. I realized that a tarot deck had seventy-eight different energies, which means a witch can use one tarot deck to cast a wide variety of spells. The cups cards can be used for love and relationship spells. Cards in the pentacles suit can be used for money spells. Wands are perfect for career spells. Swords are excellent for problem-solving and new ideas spells. And that's just the beginning of the magical intentions tarot cards can represent.

Calling in the Quarters

If you are planning on performing some serious magic, you might want to call in the quarters. This is a ritual many witches will do before casting a major spell. Calling in the quarters (sometimes referred to as "calling in the corners") can create a circle of protection around a witch or to add power to a spell. I like doing this if I want to conjure up a big gush of energy.

To call in the quarters, take a moment to orient yourself. Identify what direction is north and face that way as begin. I use the compass app on my iPhone to do this. Next, select four tarot cards—one to represent each element (earth, water, fire, and air). Each tarot card can correspond with a particular element—some can be used for multiple elements. You can choose cards intuitively or you can use some ideas from the list below!

To start, place the card you've chosen to represent earth so that it faces north on your altar and invite that element to your magical practice. You can say something like, "Earth to the North, please lend your energy to my magic today." Do the same thing with the other three elements.

Here's the traditional order to call in the quarters. It's written as counter-clockwise because that's the direction of the earth's rotation. However, you're totally welcome to do it in a different order. Do whatever feels most natural.

Order For Inviting The Elements
First: Earth to the North
Second: Water to the West
Third: Fire to the South
Fourth: Air to the East

When your magic is complete, dismiss the elements one at a time with a thank you. (For example: "Thank you, Earth, for sharing your energy with me. Go if you wish!" Whatever order you called the elements in, dismiss each one in reverse order.

Order For Dismissing The Elements
First: Air to the East
Second: Fire to the South
Third: Water to the West
Fourth: Earth to the North

Elements and their Corresponding Directions
Earth—North
Water—West
Fire—South
Air—East

Tarot Cards by Element:

Note: This is not a complete list, and I invite you to experiment with your own correspondences based on your perception of the tarot cards! Don't let this list box you in.

Any Element:

The Magician

The Fool

Earth:

Any cards in the pentacles suit

The Empress

The Emperor

The World

Water:

Any cards in the cups suit

Temperance

The Star

The Moon

Fire:

Any cards in the wands suit

The Lovers

The Chariot

The Sun

Air:

Any cards in the swords suit

The High Priestess

The Hierophant

The Hermit

Death

How To Use Tarot Cards for Spells

For general spells, all you need to do is decide on the intention for your spell. Write the intention on a piece of paper and place that paper on your altar. I've gotten the best results with intentions that are written in the first person, present tense, and with a focus on the positive. For example, if you're doing a money spell you could use an intention like, "I have more than enough money for all my desires."

That intention may be more powerful than something like, "I will get rid of my credit card debt."

Though that intention is written in the first person, it is written in the future tense and with a focus on debt rather than an abundance of money. For more info on wording spells, check out my other book in this series, How To Become A Witch.

Once you have your intention written down, choose a card (or a few cards) to correspond and add power to that specific intention.

For ideas, check out this list below. Just remember, this list is by no means complete, and I firmly believe you should listen to your intuition above all else. If you feel drawn to a particular card, follow that nudge! The intention you put behind a particular card is more important than the traditional meaning of the card.

Tarot Cards For Specific Magical Intentions

For money, financial abundance, and new jobs

- The Empress
- The World
- Ace of Pentacles
- Page of Pentacles
- Three of Pentacles
- Nine of Pentacles
- Ten of Pentacles
- King of Wands
- Four of Wands
- Three of Wands
- Six of Wands

For romantic love, self love, friendships, and other relationships

- The Lovers
- Ace of Cups
- Two of Cups
- Six of Cups
- Four of Wands

For strengthening intuition and connecting to your higher power or higher wisdom

- The High Priestess
- The Empress
- The Hierophant
- The Hermit
- The Wheel of Fortune
- Death
- The Star
- The Moon
- Eight of Cups

For luck and wishes

- The Fool
- The Magician
- The Star
- The Sun
- Ace of Wands
- Six of Wands
- Eight of Wands

For releasing unwanted energy

- Justice
- The Wheel of Fortune

- The Hanged Man
- Death
- The Tower
- The Star
- Judgment
- Eight of Cups
- The High Priestess
- Ace of Swords

For productivity

- The Emperor
- The Chariot
- Two of Pentacles
- Three of Pentacles
- King of Wands
- Ace of Wands
- Three of Wands
- Eight of Wands
- Queen of Wands
- King of Wands
- Ace of Swords
- Knight of Swords

For emotional healing

- The Empress

- Strength
- Temperance
- The Star
- Ace of Cups
- Queen of Cups
- The High Priestess
- Eight of Cups

How to Position Your Cards on Your Altar

To add power and sharpen your intention, you can arrange your cards in a specific shape that represents something to you. Just like choosing your cards, you should always follow your intuition when positioning your tarot cards.

Power Triangle Spell

This shape is what I use for most of my tarot spells. Three is a powerful number in magic, and the points of the triangle can be positioned to direct that power towards something or someone. I usually angle the bottom point of the triangle towards myself to draw the magic towards me.

For this spellcasting spread, choose three cards. One tarot card will represent you. Often this is the Fool, but it can also be any card you feel drawn to. This card goes at the bottom point of the triangle. Next, pick one tarot card that represents the energy of your intention. For example: a pentacles card would be great for a manifesting money spell. This card goes to the upper left of the triangle. The left side is associated with receiving energy, which is perfect for calling in money, or whatever your intention is. The right corner of the triangle is for sending out energy. Pick whatever card you feel would help you make your intention a reality. Think of this card as sending up the energy needed to support your intention. For example: if you want to attract money by getting a promotion at work, you can use the Three of Pentacles, the Emperor, or the Page of Pentacles to support that intention. You can meditate in front of your spellcasting spread. I like to visualize myself experiencing my ideal outcome for my spell as I sit near my altar. You can also leave this spread up under the moonlight. Full moons are excellent for manifesting spells.

Manifesting Circle Tarot Spread

This tarot spell casting spread is super fun. Circles represent birth, life cycles, transformation, and creation, which is great energy for a manifesting spell or any spell where you're trying to take an idea and make it a reality. It's a nice-looking spread to use in a big room or an outside space because you can make the circle as big or small as you want.

To do this spellcasting spread, go through your

cards with your intention in mind and select cards you think would support your spell. (Refer to the list above if you need ideas!) This spell can use any number of cards. Maybe you want to use a number that holds some kind of significance, like seven, eleven, or thirteen. Maybe you just want to pick cards until you feel complete. Either approach works! Once you have your cards, arrange them in a circle in any order. You can place the Fool card in the center to represent yourself. I also like to write my intention down on a piece of paper and place it inside the circle. You might feel some extra power if you sit inside the circle and let the cards surround you with their magic.

Activating the Magic of Your Tarot Spell

After you've set up your tarot spread for spellwork, you can proceed with your spell the way you normally would. I usually set up my tarot cards and sit quietly for ten to twenty minutes, visualizing my intention. If you prefer journaling about your intention, spend that time writing out the details of your desire. Then place your journal or journal pages on top of the cards or in the center of the spread you've created. You can also burn candles, set up a tiny cauldron to diffuse essential oil, or place a crystal in the center of your spread while you meditate.

A Sentimental Tarot Love Spell

Love magic (self-love, romantic love, friendship, etc) is one of the most popular types of spells to perform. I've had some amazing results from my love magic. One time, after doing five days of morning love visualizations in a row, I got a string of text messages, phone calls, and social media messages from all of my exes. I'm not even kidding. Every. Single. One. My friends thought it was hilarious and called it "the Ex-Boyfriend Parade." It was a strange experience, but it reaffirmed my belief in magic.

Sometimes love spells have a bad reputation because some witches have ended up turning someone into a stalker or making him or her obsess over the spellcaster. No one wants that! Another common complaint with love spells is that some witches will end up doing love spells for someone they decide they're not into a week later.

The good thing about this love spell is that its intention is to make someone think of you. It doesn't force them to love you or obsess over you. Think of it as a cosmic text message sent through the ether.

If you want to explore love magic in a safe, healthy way, here's a fun tarot spell to try!

What You'll Need:

- A candle (optional)
- A crystal (optional)
- Objects that remind you of the person you want to think of you
- A tarot deck

Directions:

Step One: Create a sacred space. Do this by placing several objects around you that make you think of the person you're trying to connect with. This can be a picture of them, an old movie ticket stub from a movie you saw together, or an object in their favorite color.

Use a crystal or candle as a focal point on your altar or in your sacred space if you like.

Crystals that will support this intention are:

- Clear quartz
- Blue apatite
- Carnelian
- Rose quartz
- Amethyst
- Selenite
- Citrine

Candle colors that support this intention are:

- Red
- Pink
- Purple
- White
- The person's favorite color

If you don't have a specific color, use whatever is on hand. I'm a firm believer that the most important part of your magic is always your intention.

Step Two: Light the candle. Practice fire safety when you do this and never leave a candle unattended.

Step Three: Go through your tarot deck and pull out three cards.

-A card that represents you

-A card that represents the person you want to think of you

For those two cards, almost any of the Major

Arcana cards will work. I often use cards like the Empress, Emperor, the Magician, the High Priestess, and the Fool.

-A card that represents the relationship you want to cultivate between the two of you —Two of Cups, Ten of Cups, Nine of Cups, or almost any cups card will work!

If you would rather ask your deck what cards best represent you, your person, and the relationship you'd like to cultivate, feel free to shuffle and draw cards from the tarot deck rather than selecting them yourself.

Step Four: Arrange your cards in front of you. Place your left hand on the card that represents the person you want to think of you. Place your right hand on the card that represents you.

Step Five: Begin your visualization. Visualize this person wherever he or she is right now in the world. See this person pause in the middle of whatever they are doing and look at their phone. Visualize them opening up a social media app or their contacts and scrolling to your name or your profile.

Step Six: Make sure you connect your mind, body, and emotions to this visualization.

Think about what this person looks like, where they are, and what they are doing. Don't overthink this. Just go with the first image that appears in your mind.

Allow yourself to savor the joy and excitement

of what it feels like to have this person thinking about you so fondly.

Notice any physical sensations that rise up in your body like butterflies in your stomach or your heart rate increasing.

Stay in this visualization until you are fully immersed in it. This can be anywhere from five to fifteen minutes. Don't go longer than that. It's usually unnecessary.

Step Seven: In your mind's eye, see this person smile at the thought of you.

Step Eight: Open your eyes. Blow out your candle (or snuff it out, whatever your practice is) and your spell is complete!

Step Nine: If you want to go a step further, perform this six-card tarot spread.

Card One: What does this person think of me?

Card Two: What does this person feel for me?

Card Three: What do I think of this person?

Card Four: What do I feel for this person?

Card Five: What is the current nature of our relationship?

Card Six: What energy must I embody to improve this relationship?

A Powerful Tarot Money Spell

This is a tarot spell I've done time and time again. It has won me money in a raffle, gotten me a long-term freelance writing job, and helped me sell my old car for more than I ever thought I'd get for it.

What You'll Need:

- One piece of paper currency
- A sheet of paper and a writing utensil
- An assortment of coins, green crystals, or pieces of pyrite
- The Nine of Pentacles tarot card
- The Magician tarot card
- The King of Wands
- A green or gold birthday candle
- A black birthday candle (If you don't have

these candle colors, use whatever you have on hand. The intention is the most important part here.)

• A fireproof container (such as a cookie sheet, foil, agate slab, or something you can burn a candle on)

• A lighter

Directions:

Step One: Set the mood for magic

There are several ways you can do this, but to make this simple, I'll share just one way to prepare your space for magic.

Gather all your magical materials together and get in a comfortable position where you won't be disturbed for about thirty minutes. If the weather's nice, you can do this outside under the moon. Play some soothing music and have a comforting beverage nearby to sip on if that helps you feel relaxed.

Close your eyes and visualize in your mind's eye a white cloud of light floating down from the sky. Feel it touch the crown of your head. Notice what sensations come up as this white light touches you. Does it tingle? Is it warming? Cooling? No sensation at all? Whatever your experience is fine. Don't judge it or try to force it.

Visualize the white light moving down through your body, relaxing every inch of you as it does.

When it reaches your feet, allow it to spread out over your magical materials and fill the room.

This is the white light of the universe. By summoning it, you're cleansing and charging yourself, your magical tools, and the space.

When you sense the room is fully cleansed and charged, open your eyes. You're ready to do some magic!

Step Two: Prepare your space

Place the paper currency in the upper center of your ritual space. Arrange your tarot cards or oracle cards so the King of Wand and the Nine of Pentacles are on either side of the paper currency, and the Magician is in the middle in front of the paper currency. Put your cookie sheet, foil, agate slab, or fireproof tray in front of the Magician card. (If you don't have tarot cards, write the names of these cards on paper and place them in their positions OR use three oracle cards that you associate with financial abundance. Set your coins in a circle around your cards and paper currency. Don't worry about the number of coins or the spacing, just make sure you complete the circle.

Step Three: Write your intention

Take a couple minutes to get very clear on what you desire. Is it money? If so, what KIND of money? Do you want to win this money or make this money through a job? Maybe you want a new car rather than money. In that case, make your intention about the car rather than the money.

When you have a good idea of what exactly you want, write your intention on the sheet of paper. Fold the paper up and place it in the center near the paper currency. Intentions are strongest when they are written in first person, present-tense. It also helps to add some kind of time frame as well.

Here are a few intentions I've used for money spells:

- "Starting now, money flows to me quickly, easily, and abundantly."
- "I always have enough money for all my desires."
- "This month, I make an abundance of money working from home."
- "I drive my new mint Chevy Spark to my fourth of July BBQ."
- "This spring, I travel to a vineyard in Italy with my significant other."

Step Four: Charge your black candle

Hold your black candle between your palms. Close your eyes and think about any doubts, worries, and fears you have about getting your desire. I call these blocks, and it's helpful to identify these before you start your ritual.

For example: If your goal is to make an abundance of money from home, but you are worried your family will judge you for not going out and getting a "real" job, that's a block.

Or if it's "I always have enough money for all my desires," but all you can think about is that balance on your Mastercard, that's a block.

Maybe it's something more subtle, like you don't think you deserve money or you feel bad about wanting money when there are others who have even less than you. Those are both blocks.

Remember, it's totally fine to have these blocks. The goal here is to identify them. Once you've done that, spend two minutes visualizing all your fears, worries, and doubts sinking into the black candle that you're holding between your palms. Get those blocks out of your mind, body, and heart and put them into that candle.

Carefully melt the bottom of the black candle, allowing a bit of wax to drip onto your fireproof tray or surface. Stick the candle upright in the melted wax. Wait a few seconds for the wax to dry and let go of the candle. Hopefully, it's standing upright. If not, repeat that process again.

Once you've got it, light the candle.

Step Five: Charge and light your green or gold candle

Hold your gold or green candle between your palms. Spend two minutes visualizing your desire. Connect with your emotions here. What do you expect to feel when you have financial abundance?

Relief? Joy? Freedom? Send all those positive, glowy feelings into your candle. Adhere your candle to the fireproof surface like you did with the black one and light the candle.

Step Six: Connect to the energy of your magical tools.

Gaze at the candles as they burn. The black candle is for clearing and banishing. It is burning away your worries, doubts, and fears. The green or gold candle is sending your desire up into the universe.

Bring your gaze to the King of Wands card. Acknowledge and absorb his energy of enthusiasm, brilliant ideas, ambition, and charm. His energy will allow you to recognize when your opportunity to get your desire appears to you.

Draw your gaze toward the Nine of Pentacles. The energy of this card is wealth, luxury, abundance, and ease. Bask in the peaceful energy of this card as the candles burn.

Bring your gaze to the Magician. This is the energy that takes your idea or desire and manifests it into the physical world. You are the magician right now, taking action to turn your intention into your reality.

For the rest of the burn time, continue to visualize what your life will look like once your desire has manifested. Use all five of your senses. What do you smell, taste, hear, touch, and see? These details all work together to strengthen the power of your intention.

Step Seven: Complete your ritual.

Before the green or gold candle goes out, light your intention paper on fire and drop it into your fireproof container. Let it burn completely. This sends your intention into the universe (and the spirit world). Safely discard the ashes.

Wait for the candles to burn out on their own. Never leave these candles unattended. This process takes about thirty minutes. Thank yourself for doing the ritual. Thank your intuition, your higher power, your spirit guides, or the universe for co-creating your desires with you.

Your spell is complete! Do this spell once a week until your desire has manifested.

A Note From Julie Wilder

Thanks for picking up this book! I hope it helped you on your magical journey.

If you want to learn more ways to practice simple, secular witchcraft, be sure to pick up **a free copy of my book of spells and my free Beginner Witch Starter kit with printables, correspondences, meditations, and magical journaling prompts.** Use the link below to get both of those!

https://whitewitchacademy.com/freebies

Also, be sure to check out the other witchy books in the **White Witch Academy Textbook series.** You can find them here:

https://whitewitchacademy.com/books

If you're on social media,

follow me on Instagram or Tik Tok **@whitewitchacademy**

Or send me an email at julie@magicalpowerwithin.com

Lastly, **if you enjoyed this book leave a review so other witches can decide if this book is for them!** Reviews help me out so much and I appreciate the feedback.

Thank you for reading. I hope this book brought a little joy and magic to your life!

Until next time,

Julie Wilder xx

Also by Julie Wilder

What Type of Witch Are You?
How to Become A Witch
Why Didn't My Spell Work?
Beginner Witch's Guide to Grimoires
Tarot for Beginner Witches
Simple Moon Magic
White Witch Academy Books 1-3 Boxed Set

Printed in Great Britain
by Amazon